Unleash the Sloth! ™

Unleash the Sloth! ™

75 Ways to Reach Your Maximum Potential By Doing Less

by Rob Dircks

Illustrated by Dave Dircks

GOLDFINCH PUBLISHING

goldfinchpublishing.com

Published by Goldfinch Publishing
An Imprint of SARK Industries, Inc.
www.unleashthesloth.com
www.goldfinchpublishing.com

Publisher's Note:
This publication is designed to provide entertainment
only. It is sold with the understanding that the publisher
is not engaged in rendering professional services.
If expert assistance is required, the service of the
appropriate professional should be sought.

Library of Congress Cataloging-in-Publication Data
Rob Dircks, 1967-
Unleash the Sloth!™ 75 Ways to Reach Your Maximum
Potential By Doing Less / by Rob Dircks
p. cm.
ISBN 978-0615659268

Manufactured in the USA

First:

A Fable.

A rabbit was taking a quick rest in the shade one afternoon, and noticed a sloth hanging from a high tree branch. Irritated by how slow the creature was moving, he called up in a loud voice, "Hey! How do you ever expect to win a race moving that slow?" The sloth thought for a long moment, and replied, "What's a race?"

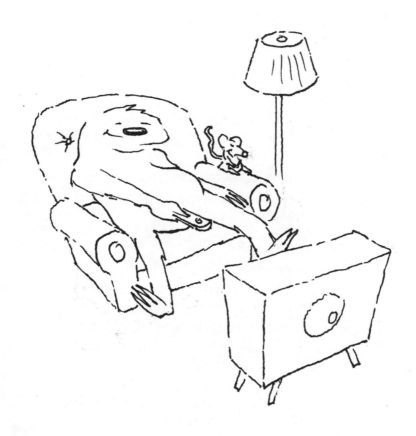

An Introduction:

Tapping Into Your Inner Sloth

Think about this for a minute: why does everything that's supposedly good for us take so much EFFORT?

Working out. Eating a healthy diet. Going to a job eight hours a day. Folding our laundry. Wiping our butts. (Okay, that last one's worth the effort.)

Now think about all the things you WANT to do, but feel like you're not supposed to. Laying on the couch and watching TV for five hours. Laying on the couch and playing video games. Laying on the couch and napping. Laying on the couch and... well, you get the idea.

So – are you starting to see the problem? **We're actually working against our own nature to reach some "potential" we didn't even get to define.**

Who says a self-help book has to be about EFFORT? **Not me.**

Within these double-spaced, large-type, easy-read pages you'll find the secret to your potential: **that like the mighty sloth, you're already hardwired to become your best – simply by letting go and *being* yourself.**

No workouts required.

In fact, your inborn laziness, underachievement, and poor goal-setting abilities are actually powerful allies in the attainment of your personal maximum potential.

I'll show you what I mean. According to Wikipedia (a Sloth™-Approved Resource), the Buddha describes reaching potential – or "Nirvana" – as *"a mind that has come to a point of perfect lucidity and clarity due to the absence of volitional formations."* Okay, I had no idea what that meant either, so I asked around. And I *think* he means that our perfect state is the bliss of desiring nothing. Now, can you name three things that require no work and create bliss? I can:

• Napping on the couch during a baseball game
• Moaning after a large meal
• Taking a thirty-minute shower

So there you have it: no pain, all gain. It's the way of the sloth, and it can be yours, too. But wait – aren't sloths lazy and useless?

No! Sure, they've been maligned for centuries, even making the Seven Deadly Sins list. But we can learn a great truth from these "gods of the trees" – **how to reach our absolute highest potential**. And if you need some convincing, just look at the stats:

- Sloths never exercise, boasting an impressive 50% _less_ muscle tissue than other animals.

- Sloths sleep from 15 to 18 hours each day. I only did that once, after a crystal-meth binge.

- Sloths move only when necessary and even then very slowly. (Maximum speed? A blazing 5 feet per minute.)

- Sloths eat their young if they do anything too fast or ambitious.

- Sloths can camouflage themselves as coconuts. (I swear I didn't make that one up.)

- As much as two-thirds of a well-fed sloth's body-weight consists of the contents of its stomach.

- Sloths were considered gods by the ancient Aztecs. (I *did* make that one up. And the "gods of the trees" thing. And the eating their young thing. But the rest I got straight from Wikipedia, so they must be true.)

In short, sloths are way ahead of us on
the road to reaching maximum potential.
It's time to catch up!

The Ways

There's only one rule for reading this book and applying the Ways in your life: DO NOT try to read too much at once. I would nap *(Way #3)*, or even leave entire weeks between Ways. Don't strain yourself. Remember: doing as little as possible is the point.

Let's get started.

Stage 1:
Learning to Hang.

"Sloths move only when necessary.
And even then very slowly."

– Wikipedia

Way #1:

Procrastinate.

Okay, let's unleash the most important Way first. (So we're prepared to procrastinate through the remaining seventy-four.)

Why feel guilty about putting things off until the absolute last second? Do you realize how **efficient** you become when you procrastinate? Instead of spending three weeks doing that accounting report, you get it done the night before – and thus save yourself three weeks minus one day. *Bravo!* Just like the mighty sloth, you've minimized your effort to get results.

Step-by-step instructions:

1. Ponder that report you're supposed to finish.

2. Don't do it.

3. At the last minute, panic and do it.

The No-Guilt Twist™:

4. Enjoy the hours, days, or even years spent procrastinating, and congratulate yourself for saving time and trusting your animal instincts.

Way #2:

Have At Least Forty Hobbies.

I know, this one sounds like a paradox. If you have lots of interests, aren't you always busy? But ironically, **the more hobbies you have, the less you actually engage in any particular one.**

For example, I have a friend who's really into skiing. Not art, music, or even other sports – just skiing. So he goes all the time, like twenty times a winter. I, on the other hand, include skiing among my fifty or so interests. So guess how many times I've been skiing? Never. Not once. *What an effort-free hobby!*

Step-by-step instructions:

1. Create a list of at least forty things you're interested in.

2. Keep working on the list, refining it over the years.

3. Don't actually do anything on the list.

HOWEVER: If any *Unleash The Sloth!* Ways are on your list – particularly **Way #17: Watching TV** – feel free to indulge in these activities as much as you want. They've already been researched, tested, and verified to require a minimum of effort.

Way #3:

Nap.

(a.k.a. "meditation")

Think all those bald monks are meditating? Ha. They're on the road to true enlightenment: **extra sleep**.

And now you can fool the world into thinking you're meditating too, grasshopper. It's simple, and you've been doing it your whole life: in the back of chemistry class, after lunch at your desk, or when your mom calls you from Florida and wants to talk for an hour.

Step-by-step instructions:

1. Wherever you are, just put your hand on your forehead, sort of covering your eyes.

2. Sleep.

3. Don't snore, or you'll give it away.

Oh, And Just In Case™:

4. Say this to anyone who calls you on it: "Thanks a lot, I was just praying for you!"

Way #4:
Don't Sort Your Laundry.

Colors? Darks? Whites? Who cares? I'm willing to bet that your dying thought *won't* be "gee, I really shouldn't have put that new red shirt in with my white underpants."

Relax. Consider yourself a non-conformist. A trend-setter. And why do you think they make those washing machines so big anyway – to fit little, perfectly-sorted mini-loads? Nope.

Step-by-step instructions:

1. Throw all your dirty laundry into one load. (Or, for *Advanced Learners, replace with alternate Step 1: Avoid doing laundry completely.*)

2. Do NOT put in bleach.

3. Flip back and forth a few times through a magazine.

The No-Guilt Twist™:

4. Think about all the water you're conserving. All the bleach you're not releasing into the environment. All that extra time for Halo 3.

And when you're done...

Way #5:

Put Clothes Directly from Dryer to Drawer.

People get *paid* for folding clothes at The Gap. Why should you do it for FREE? You're just going to wear it again anyway, right? Save yourself hours over your lifetime by stuffing your clean clothes back into your dresser drawers where they belong.

Step-by-step instructions:

1. Grab an armful of clean laundry.

2. Cram it into your first available dresser drawer.

3. Stop when you can barely close the drawer.

4. Repeat with other drawers until the only exposed laundry is the new dirty pile of clothes on the floor.

The No-Guilt Twist™:

5. Tell anyone who notices that wrinkles are the new black.

Oh, And Just In Case™:

Got a date? Put on a sport coat. And if you MUST look your best, just iron the little bit of shirt that peeks out.

Way #6:

Wait in Line.

If you find waiting in a line annoying, you're just thinking about it backwards – it's not keeping you from doing something better. It's keeping you from having to do *anything!* The benefits in detail:

- It frees you temporarily from the other harsh demands of life. (Don't worry, they'll still be there when you're done waiting.)
- It requires NO effort.
- It gives you time to daydream (Way #55) or stare off into space (Way #56).
- And if you're lucky, it even gives you time to watch bad television on a dusty, 10-year-old set hanging from a drop-ceiling at the local DMV.

My favorite lines (in favoriteness order):

1. **Department of Motor Vehicles.** This is my favorite because when I get to the front, there's always something they say I forgot, so I have to go fill out another form and then proceed to the back of the line. *Yay! More waiting!*

2. **It's a Small World Ride at DisneyWorld.** This is my second favorite because you can easily wait for an hour to see styrofoam marionettes

dance to the famous mind-numbing jingle over and over – and over. And then at some other point on your trip, you inexplicably find yourself on that same line again.

3. **The security check line at Dulles International Airport on a Friday afternoon.** Holy crap – THIS is a line. Also one of my favorites, because when it makes me miss my flight, I have *even more* time to loiter.

3. **Traffic Court.** This is one of my favorites because it's a symphony of different lines, rooms, and friendly people to talk to. And it easily blows an entire day. *Thank you for that speeding ticket, officer!*

Way #7:
Double-space your work.

Why fill pages with words? Some famous writer once said "Write less. Say more." *(I can't remember his name, and I don't feel like doing research. If you find out that no one actually said that, please scribble in a "©2012 Rob Dircks" for me, okay?)*

I'll prove how few words we actually need to get a whole story with this example:

"To be or not to be? That is the question."

Do you remember ANY other lines from *Hamlet*? Do you NEED to? No. Those two lines tell the entire epic: everyone apparently answers the question with "not to be," and (spoiler alert) dies at the end.

Try This Experiment!™:

Now it's time for your liberation from the pressure of single-spacing and word vomiting:

1. Stare at the next six blank pages for 15 minutes.

2. Stop staring. It's creeping me out.

3. Write a single word on each page that forms a six word sentence. (You can use *"To be or not to be"* if you don't want to strain yourself.)

4. Bask in the glory of simplicity you've just created.

This page left intentionally blank
for your *Try This Experiment!*™

This page left intentionally blank
for your *Try This Experiment!*™

This page left intentionally blank
for your *Try This Experiment!*™

This page left intentionally blank
for your *Try This Experiment!*™

This page left intentionally blank
for your *Try This Experiment!*™

This page left intentionally blank
for your *Try This Experiment!*™

Way #8:

Take Short Cuts.

Okay, let's say you're writing a book, and your editor tells you you're six pages short. Hmmm. What the heck do you do with all that blank space? You guessed it – Make up a *Try This Experiment!*™ *(See last six pages.)*

Other examples of valuable short cuts:

- You know that one way street that would shave five minutes off your commute if you could just make it a two-way street? Make your dream come true today.

- Guess wildly at your tax deductions. Adding up all those receipts is a torture rightly reserved for anal-retentive number-crunchers, not you.

- Instead of actually reading, flip back and forth a few times through a magazine or book to get the general idea. You're not being graded, right? (And if someone IS grading you, you're in school and should be reading *Unleash The Sloth for Students* instead. Now get back to class!)

Way #9:

Get Sick.

Admit it. There's at least some little part of you that loves the idea of shirking every responsibility, curling up in your bed all day, and periodically moaning like a wounded moose.

This Way is extremely effective at reaching a state of sloth-inspired potential because it incorporates several other Ways:
- Napping   • Sleeping In   • Watching TV
- Ducking Responsibility   • Playing Video Games

Because of its complex nature, the art of getting sick requires practice. This isn't like faking a fever in the fourth grade – this is actual, but not painful, sickness. *Be careful.*

Step-by-step instructions:

1. Casually walk around a hospital. Shake as many hands as possible. Step in front of someone's sneeze spray if possible.

2. Get sick. (Not too sick. Just sick enough to stay home, sleep a lot, and get some well deserved sympathy).

3. Get better. (Resist the temptation to linger in your illness. You'll stop getting sympathy. And lose your job. And die.)

Way #10:
Do All Your Research on Wikipedia.

Man, I'm still pissed they didn't have Wikipedia when I went to high school. Can you imagine how many more hours I could've logged on *Space Invaders* if I didn't have to actually look for facts in books and – please kill me – **microfiche?**

Well, although a little late for me, the great gift has arrived, folks. Someone (I have no idea who, and don't care) has done all the research in the world and made it one click away – just for you. In fact, other than TV, it's probably the best tool in your Sloth Arsenal™. *Thank you, whoever!*

Step-by-step instructions:

1. Go to Wikipedia.org.

2. Type in "My Research Subject" (don't actually type those words in, unless that's what you need to find, which would be a really crazy coincidence).

3. Copy and paste into your homework.

The No-Guilt Twist™:

4. I'm not suggesting you plagiarize, of course. As long as you reference Wikipedia, it's legitimate, 100% truthful, effortless research!

Way #11:

Sleep In.

Sure, the early bird catches the worm. But worms are disgusting. I'd much rather sleep in and still be in my pajamas when *The People's Court* comes on at four o'clock in the afternoon. *(Sorry if you now have The People's Court theme song playing in your head the rest of the day.)*

Step-by-step instructions:

1. Go to bed late (preferably after Watching TV, Way #17, or Playing Video Games, Way #20)

2. Sleep.

3. When you wake up, don't get out of bed. For another four hours.

Oh, And Just In Case™:

4. If your boss calls at one o'clock wondering where the hell you are, remind him that today was your "Volunteering-for-the-Cure" day. And if he's callous enough to ask "a cure for *what*?" here are a few options:

- Icky Thump (yes, it's the name of a *White Stripes* song, but your boss won't know that.)

- Straphalapogos (try saying it without laughing)

- Parasitic Brain Eating Flu Virus Bacteria (PBEFVB)

- Ferpes (Feline Herpes – don't ask how I know that one.)

Way #12:
Duck Responsibility.

If you can't have your ultimate, effortless dream job – hand model, Caribbean vacation critic, pain medication tester – then do the next best thing: **hide**.

Just like the crafty sloth, who camouflages himself as coconuts to avoid having to actually run away from predators, there are easy ways you can avoid the enormous hassle of work:

- When you see your boss walking down the hall, make sure you're headed in the opposite direction, preferably with papers in your hand. Look determined, like you're on your way to delivering the quarterly earnings report to the press.

- Volunteer other people. Here's a sample: "Listen, Ted... Sheri's really been inspiring the way she talks about keeping reports up-to-date. She's a natural."

- Don't be afraid to be bad at things! If your reports are sub-par, Ted will go right past you to Sheri. (Although it helped that you volunteered her, too.)

- **Do NOT keep a clean desk.** Nothing says "give me more responsibility" than empty space. Instead, place giant stacks of work-looking stuff on your desk. People will be afraid to overload you with that one more thing they need. (It helps if you sigh and point to the stack when they ask, too.) Remember, however, to rotate the stuff, or bright co-workers might catch on.

Way #13:

Replace Your Signature with an "X."

Not only will it be FUN to slash at checks and business forms like Zorro, but just imagine the hand-cramping pain you'll never have to endure again (*okay, that sounds like an infomercial, sorry*). Or the hours (*okay, minutes*) saved by not writing out *Robert Andrew Theodore Dircks* for the rest of your life.

Seriously – let's say your name is *James Smith*. A pretty short name. But it's still got <u>ten</u> characters in it, compared to <u>one</u> in the letter X. **That's a 90% reduction in signing effort!**

Step-by-step instructions:

1. Grasp the target document.

2. Grasp a writing instrument.

3. Scribble a big "X" anywhere on the paper as quickly as possible.

And Just For Good Measure™:

4. Wink at the person you're presenting the document to, like a pirate who just drew the X on his latest treasure map.

Way #14:

Do You REALLY Want Kids?

Now, I love kids. I've got two of my own. But if the maximum potential of "nothingness" is at the target end of the spectrum, then kids are at the exact opposite end – they're like "everythingness." These little balls of energy will sap your life force, make you go to their baseball games, take all your money to buy churros at their baseball games, ask you a billion questions every night right before bed, and wake you up at 6:30am on the weekends.

Step-by-step instructions:

1. Do each of the following:
    a) Go to an Applebee's at 7pm on a Friday night.
    b) Crash a birthday party at Chuck E. Cheese's.
    c) Change a diaper.
    d) Clean up a puddle of vomit.

2. Ask yourself "Do I really want kids?"

3. If the answer is still "yes," congratulations! (I think.)

And if you do find yourself with offspring...

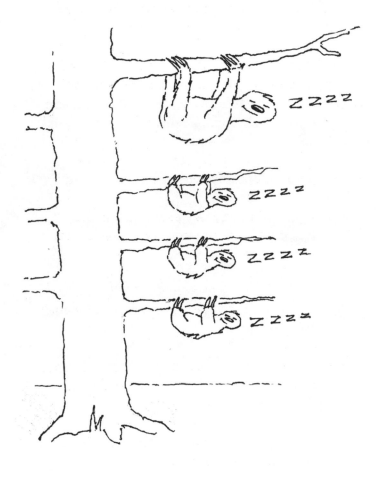

zzzz

zzzz

zzzz

zzzz

Way #15:
Teach Your Kids the Ways.

Of course it's okay to have as many kids as you want. BUT if you do, help them become the next Sloth Generation by passing down the valuable lessons you've learned so far in life:

- Watching too much TV is bad – so break it up by playing video games for a few hours before you go back to the *Spongebob* marathon you were watching.

- Racing through your homework is good because it teaches you to trust your instincts.

- Making your bed is a waste of time, since you're going to jump into it in a few hours anyway.

- Chores are for Alice from *The Brady Bunch*. (Your kids won't get the reference, but they'll thank you anyway.)

- Washing your hands is also a waste of time, because it prevents your body from building up its immune system.

- Forgetting to flush the toilet is actually good, because it conserves water.

And if you have more than one kid, here's a sure-fire way to simplify your life...

Way #16:

Give All Your Kids
The Same Name.

That's right – I don't care if it's five boys and three girls. Name them all *Terry* and the benefits just keep adding up:

- Save yourself a lifetime of remembering who's who. Bobby, Timmy, Sue, Jill, John, and Spencer? What a hassle.

- Makes it much easier to call everyone into the dining room for dinner.

- Dole out punishments in a snap. No more "Johnny did it" or "Sue did it." No more finding out who's to blame so that you're always fair. It's "Terry did it, so you're all grounded for a week."

- Save time writing your will. Terry gets everything! (And don't worry yourself over the family infighting of five Terrys – you won't be around to deal with it.)

Stage 2:
Drifting Off.

A sloth walks into the doctor's office. "Doc, I'm having trouble sleeping. I can't seem to get twelve in a row."

"You need twelve hours?"

"No. Days."

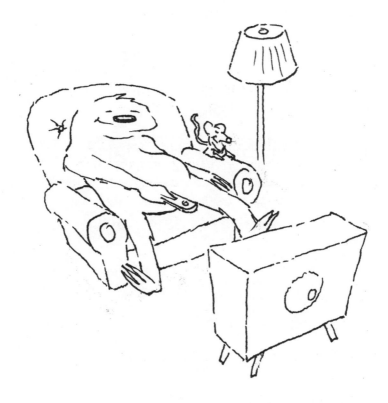

The sloth's body has evolved over millennia to perfectly fit the contours of a La-Z-Boy recliner.

Way #17:

Watch TV.

Possibly the king of all Ways, the venerable television is virtually a one-stop shop to reaching your true sloth potential.

Imagine – someone actually invented a box that requires us to do NOTHING but sit there and absorb limitless quantities of valuable entertainment and information.

I can't even begin to calculate the enjoyment earned and effort saved by watching hours of TV a day instead of being productive. (Because trying to calculate that would take me away from my *Seinfeld* reruns.)

Step-by-step instructions:

1. Sit.

2. Click.

3. Absorb.

4. *(Optional but recommended)* Snack.

The No-Guilt Twist™:

Do you have any idea how many reality shows are on TV? And they're like documentaries, which are good for you. *Enlightenment, here we come!*

Way #18:

Be Apathetic.

Sounds counter-intuitive, right? But there it is, in all the self-help books: the more you treasure the things of this world, the more trapped you become.

So it's time for your liberation, and the way is simple – **stop giving a crap**.

Oh, and by the way, releasing yourself from desire is another thing those bald monks practice. And that's just fancy talk for not giving a crap.

Step-by-step instructions:

1. Be apathetic.

2. You were expecting a second step?

Way #19:

Use Cruise Control Only.

Gas pedal? Really? Who needs it, when you've got little buttons you can press with your finger? You'll enjoy using it even on small trips – it makes driving infinitely more ~~dangerous~~ relaxing.

Before your start:

1. Make sure your car insurance is paid up.

Step-by-step instructions:

2. At every green light, step on the gas pedal just enough to get you up to cruise-control speed.

3. Let your fingers take over.

4. Stretch those tired ankles. You deserve a break.

And Just For Good Measure™:

Try controlling your speed **and** your radio simultaneously for even more ~~accidents~~ fun.

Way #20:
Play Video Games.

Although this Way takes much more effort than simply Watching TV, it's worth it when you look bleary-eyed at the clock and say "Wait - did I just play *World of Warcraft* for twelve hours?"

Now **that's** Nirvana: loss of self, bliss, no sense of time, pure being. I actually wonder why modern self-help authors don't endorse it more – it satisfies all the goals of transcendental meditation, without all the breathing sounds and awkward sitting positions.

Step-by-step instructions:

1. Sit. *(You can stand for Wii, but talk about effort!)*

2. Play.

3. Miss an entire day of work.

4. Make sure your resume is up-to-date.

And Just For Good Measure™:

Have lots of snacks and caffeinated soda within arm's reach – having to actually get up and move around can shock you out of your deep trance-like state. And you might accidentally look at a clock.

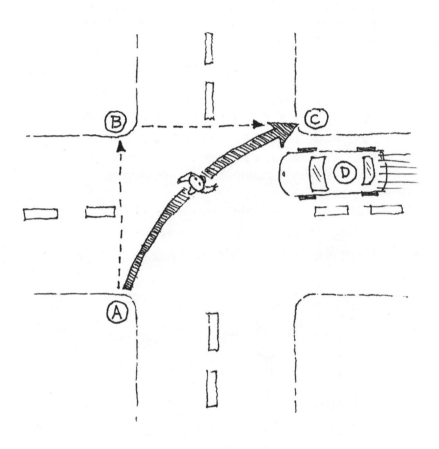

Way #21:

Jaywalk.

Unless you're in midtown Manhattan at five o'clock on a workday, jaywalking simply isn't dangerous. *(If my cousin Ted is reading this, remember it's a humor book. And I'm sorry about your legs.)*

Okay – more math. If a typical city street is 65 feet wide (that's what the Internet told me), then to get from point A to point B to point C on the map at left, you'll be walking 130 *feet!* On the other hand, if you jaywalk from point A directly to point C, you're only schlepping 92 feet (still almost long enough to take a cab, but 30% less than if you obey the law!)

Step-by-step instructions:

1. Close your **eyes**.

2. Proceed directly from point A to point C.

3. Avoid point D (that oncoming car – *watch out!*).

The No-Guilt Twist™:

4. If anyone swerves and honks to avoid you, smile and know that you're improving their *driving-while-swerving-while-honking* skills. Good job, citizen!

Way #22:
Adopt a Sloth.

I know it sounds crazy, but who better to learn idleness from – **than the master himself?** Adopt your very own, and watch as he.. um.. well, he doesn't do anything! Hang him from a lamp and go out for a walk, and when you return, he's still there! Go on a 10-day cruise, and he'll still be hanging from the damn lamp when you get back! Go on safari for three months, and he – well, you get the picture.

But how the heck do you get your hands on a *sloth?* Don't worry – I've made it almost effortless:

1. Go online and close your Facebook page.
2. Visit **www.unleashthesloth.com** and click on the *Adopt-a-Sloth*™ link.
3. Have a valid credit card handy.*
4. Wait a few weeks** and *presto!* A crate with your very own live sloth*** and a six-month supply of *Unleash The Sloth* brand sloth food**** arrives at your door.*****
5. Care for the sloth for the next 40 years.******

Oh, And Just In Case™:

If having a live, wild animal in your home (no matter how cute) just isn't your thing, you can also *Adopt-A-Sloth-The-Even-Easier-Way*™.

You don't actually get a live sloth, but a realistic plush replica. (Honestly, sometimes I can't even tell the difference.)

* That doesn't mean it has to be *your* credit card, it just has to be valid.

** We rescue sloths from the hands of villainous poachers, so we can't give you an exact delivery date. (And don't worry, we open a big can of whoop-ass on those poachers while we're at it.)

*** Sloths come ready to name! (Although I named mine *Professor DooLittle*, so if you could name yours something else I'd appreciate it.)

**** Recurring six-month food supplies will be delivered and charged to your credit card until you provide a valid death certificate for your sloth.

***** No P.O. boxes, please. Sloths are pretty small, but not *that* small.

****** I'm so certain you'll love your sloth (not named *Professor DooLittle*, please), that I'm backing it with a 100% satisfaction guarantee. If at any time during the first 40 years you decide you'd like to return your sloth, for any reason, simply package it in the original crate, call us for a SRAN (Sloth Return Authorization Number), and we'll be happy to find a loving home for the gentle, wonderful, enigmatic creature that you're now willing to cast out like an unwanted guest. *(Woah, I'm sorry about the tone – I guess I'm just really passionate about the Adopt-A-Sloth™ program. It helps keep the sloths we rescue from villuinous poachers in loving hands – except, apparently, yours. Oh, jeez - there I go again. Sorry.)*

Shower Once a Week.

When did somebody first decide that we had to shower *every day?* Come on. Save yourself the trouble and put some more deodorant on. (In my family we called it "mask odor.") Bad hair day? That's what baseball hats are for. Going on a date? Wear a blazer and don't lift your arms.

Step-by-step instructions:

1. Pick a day of the week.

2. Shower only on that day.

3. For the rest of the week, don't do anything that would make you sweat. (If you're a true student of the Ways, this should be easy.)

And Just For Good Measure™:

4. Hang out with people who bathe even less often than you, so you'll be known as the "clean one."

The No-Guilt Twist™:

Every time your own B.O. almost makes you gag, remind yourself once again how much water you're conserving. *Come on, we're saving the planet here, folks!*

If you have a treadmill, get creative: it's an excellent
place to hang laundry, pile boxes, or if you're small like
this fella, use it as a day bed.

Way #24:
Eliminate All Exercise.

Ask a sloth if he exercises. (Actually don't –
you'll be waiting a very long time for an answer.)
If he did answer, however, he'd tell you that he's
never exercised in his life – but still got around
fine, ate his fill, had a wife and kids, and lived a
happy life.

Or take a look to the great teachers in history.
Does Buddha look like he exercised? Did Jesus'
Sermon on the Mount start off with jumping
jacks? Did Ghandi pump iron? Did Martin Luther
King Jr. organize a massive iron-man triathlon
on Washington? No, no, no, and no – our best
teachers said *bupkis* about working out.

Now, If you still feel like you MUST exercise,
focus only on your hand muscles. That way you
can:

- Work the TV remote like a Jedi master.
- Lift cheese doodles to your mouth with more
  dexterity.
- Play video games better.
- Send text messages even more efficiently.
- Search faster – and get lost faster – on Google
  (*see* Way #32).

Note that all Unleash the Sloth Workshops
are attendance-optional.

Way #25:
Attend an *Unleash The Sloth!* Workshop.

(Well, I wouldn't exactly call it a "work"shop.)
Here's a peek at the sessions we're offering:

- "Procrastination: The Mother of Invention"
- "Video Game Snacking Strategies"
- "Excuses, Excuses: A Brainstorming Session"
- "Napping 'Work'shop (Bring Your Own Pillow)"
- "Sloth Care 101: How to Hang One from a Lamp"

And, in typical *Unleash The Sloth* fashion, I've made it easy to participate:

1. Go online and close your Facebook page.
2. Visit **www.unleashthesloth.com** and click on the **Sloth Workshops™** link.
3. Pick out your preferred sessions.
4. We'll mail you your completion certificate.

Wait - completion certificate? Oh, I forgot to mention: for maximum ease, I've made this an "absentee" workshop. *No attendance necessary!* Your handsome certificate, ready for framing, will allow you to show your friends and family how much you've accomplished, even as they remark, "I didn't even notice you were gone."

It's been predicted that in fifty years, our language
will consist entirely of text abbreviations and
cute symbols made from punctuation marks.

Way #26:
Text Message.

As you've hopefully realized, *Unleash the Sloth* isn't about becoming lazy – it's about doing less of what you *don't want to do,* and making what you *do want to do* even *easier.* (Okay, maybe it's a tiny little bit about becoming lazy.)

Take text messaging – sure it's fun, but why type entire sentences, when little fragments and cute abbreviations can save you valuable finger taps? Here's a quick-start guide so you can start trimming taps – and being hip – today.

LONG: I'll see you later
SHORT: **cul8tr** *(12 characters saved)*

LONG: I'm rolling on the floor laughing
SHORT: **ROFL** *(29 characters saved)*

LONG: Last night was really special. I'd like to do it again soon. Are you free this weekend?
SHORT: **me-u-humpmore?** *(63 characters saved)*

LONG: I thought we broke up a week ago, Jamie. I'll have to ask you to please not text me again.
SHORT: **fu** *(88 characters saved)*

LONG: Hey, did you hear about this new book *Unleash The Sloth?* It's a remarkable work. I'm reading it right now, and it's changing my life.
SHORT: **UtS!** *(128 characters saved!)*

Way #27:

Go to the Movies.

It's fun. It's dark. It's comfortable. You get to eat crap food. You can be with your friends and not even talk. And you don't have to lift a finger. **Win!**

Way #28:

Get a Refrigerator For Your Cubicle.

It's one thing that they expect you to work, but they also want you to walk *all the way* down to the break room to get a soda? WTF? I say **stand your ground** and show them who's boss.
(Or sit your ground, I guess.)

NOTE: if you want to heat up your cold mac and cheese from last night, you'll need a microwave in your cubicle, too.

Way #29:

Make Believe
It's Your Birthday.

It's a rule: you don't have to do anything you don't want to on your birthday. So why celebrate just once a year? I recommend doing it at least three times annually, so you can repeatedly enjoy:

- Your mom cooking your favorite meal. (Assuming you still *Live With Your Parents, Way #57*. Also assuming your mom won't catch on that your last birthday was only 4 months ago.)

- Getting to watch what you want on TV without sharing.

- Cake and soda together.

- A free Slurpee at 7-11 (if you can get away with not showing proof).

- No chores.

- Putting your feet up on the couch without getting yelled at.

WARNING: To succeed at this Way, you'll always have to be vague about telling people when your birthday is, and can never reveal the actual date. Sorry.

"Quit? I didn't even know you worked here."

Way #30:
Don't Go To Work Today.

Obviously, the less time you spend in work, the less effort you'll expend. And I know what you're saying: "That's easier said than done." Fair enough. But I'm not asking you to go AWOL. You'll need a good excuse – and I've prepared some new ones that should seem perfectly plausible:

"Sorry, I won't be able to make it in today, because... um..."

1. "... it's my birthday." *(See Way #29)*

2. "... the FBI's using my apartment to stake out the guy across the street, and they told me it would be a breach of national security to leave."

3. "... I'm having a home MRI machine delivered for my dog's serious illness (which will require even more time off, but we can talk about that when I'm back in the office tomorrow), so I have to wait for the delivery guy to come.

4. "... my kids (I know I never told you about them, but I have two) both have yellow-scarlet-black fever and they're projectile-vomiting other colors, too. Should I describe it in detail, or are we good?"

5. "... I quit."

And number five naturally leads to...

Way #31:

Don't Go To Work Ever Again.

As you can see, we're starting to get into the more serious Ways. To prepare for this one, you'll need either A) unlimited wealth; B) parents who'll let you live with them indefinitely; or C) a really strong desire to live like a hobo.

Now, there are several approaches you can take to Way #31, so you may take several years of meaningless jobs to develop your own personal style.

Approach #1 – Invisibility:

1. Over the course of the next month, stop talking to everyone, especially your boss.

2. Arrange giant piles of paperwork next to you, so on an average day your co-workers won't even be able to tell if you're at your desk.

3. Stop going to work, and see how many direct deposit paychecks you can collect before they get smart to you. *(My record was five.)*

Approach #2 – Disability:

1. Pass the civil service exam.
   (Sorry, some effort required.)

2. Apply for a position as Environmental Radiation Specialist (I swear that's a real civil service job, I looked it up).

3. Spray some glow-in-the-dark paint on yourself, claim that you got radiation poisoning, and never work another day in your life. *Booyah!*

Approach #3 – Unreliability

1. Start becoming even worse than you already are at following through with projects.

2. As you make your boss and co-workers look bad, they'll rely on you less and less (if you haven't already been fired), and eventually stop approaching your office altogether.

3. Close your office door, climb out the window, trot to the bank, and cash that paycheck!

Approach #4 – Balls

1. Walk into your boss' office.

2. Say "I quit."

3. Walk confidently out as your envious co-workers stare in awe... Then try to resist screaming in terror as you realize that hobos – even the classiest – can't afford a *World of Warcraft* subscription.

Stage 3:
The Sloth Mind.

A Buddhist monk attempts to train a sloth in the ways of transcendental meditation. "To begin," the monk whispers, "you must empty your mind."

The sloth whispers in reply, "Oh, that's easy. There wasn't anything in there to begin with."

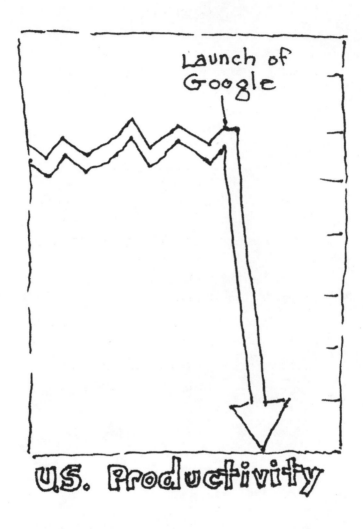

Figure 1: U.S. Productivity since inception of Google.

Way #32:

Google.

It's incredible how lost and ultimately unproductive you can be when you use the ultimate search tool. One minute you'll be innocently looking up Jeep lease prices, and twenty minutes later you're on YouTube watching a cat play the piano (for the twenty-sixth time). What a refreshing antidote for our over-achieving, overproductive world! *(See Figure 1: Productivity Chart on opposite page.)*

WARNING: when using this Way, you may find yourself doing actual work.

Step-by-step instructions:

1. Go online and close your Facebook page and/or **www.unleashthesloth.com** page.

2. Go to Google and type in your search term.

3. An hour later, ask yourself, "What the heck was I looking for in the first place?"

Doors. What a hassle.

Way #33:

Remove All the
Doorknobs in Your House.

Other than your front door (keeps out your in-laws), is there really a good reason for doorknobs? Think of the hours (okay, minutes) of wrist strain you'll avoid by simply pushing your way through the doors of your home like a Neanderthal.

(Note: this Way is especially helpful when you've got your hands full of snacks and you need to get back into your bedroom to watch TV.)

And if you find this effective...

Way #34:

Remove All the
DOORS in Your House.

Why stop at doorknobs? There's just as much waste of energy actually pushing your way into and out of rooms, so go ahead – *free yourself from friction!* (You'll also be free from that pesky little thing called privacy.)

Way #35:
Go to Church.

Relax – I'm not espousing believing in or practicing any particular faith. I'm simply pointing out an excellent place to nap.

Way #36:

Enjoy a Sunset.

I know it sounds new-agey, but you don't really have to enjoy the actual sunset. You can just enjoy the fact that the only muscle you're using is your eyes.

Way #37:

Go fishing.

All the talk about fishing being a non-activity is, thankfully, true. Drop a line in the water, look at the sunset (see previous Way), and marvel that you're actually enjoying TWO activities without moving a single muscle. *Bravo!*

"It's perfect. What is it?"

Become a Minimalist Painter.

Have you ever been to an art museum or gallery, and there's a blank canvas hanging on the wall, or it's got nothing but a couple of paint splats on it?

Whenever this happens, half of me really wants to appreciate what the artist is trying to say. But the other half usually wins out, and I grumble "Hey, that guy did practically nothing, and he's rich and famous. I could do that!"

Well, get ready for riches and fame – for like the mighty sloth, you too **can** do almost nothing and reach your potential as a cutting-edge modern minimalist painter!

Step-by-step instructions:

1. Buy a blank canvas. (Bigger is more impressive.)

2. Spill some paint on it. (Optional.)

3. Wait for international art-world acclaim.

Buy Yourself a Nice Throw.

Like a cape for sloth superheroes, a comfy lambswool blanket possesses incredible power. It can paralyze you the moment you slip under it, inducing a semi-hibernation state. (Strangely and luckily, it still allows your right hand to work the buttons on the remote.)

Way #40:
Set Your Pet Free.*

I know you love your pet. He's cute, cuddly, and the only one who leaps into your arms when you come home from work. (Unless you have a cat – then he slinks away from you in disdain.) But all that cuteness and fur comes at a steep price. Here, take a look at the pros and cons:

PROS:
1. Can be loved
2. Can be laughed at when doing something dumb

CONS:
1. Vet bills
2. Needs walks (midnight, in the snow, at -7°F)
3. Needs crap picked up
4. Endless vacuuming of hair
5. Licks own genitals then licks your face
6. Need supply of lint rollers
7. All furniture becomes scratch posts
8. Carpet urine
9. Cost of fancy pet bed with embroidered name
10. Cost of taxidermy (optional)

So unclip that leash, open that front door, and proudly watch your pet run and seek out their natural habitat – the woods, the shore, or that dumpster behind the mexican restaurant.

But fear not. If you simply can't kick the pet habit...

* Unless your pet is a sloth, in which case you kick ass!

If you can't adopt a sloth at <u>unleashthesloth.com</u>
(though I can't see why not), get the other pet that
requires the absolute minimum of care – a fish.

Way #41:

If You <u>Must</u> Have a Pet, Get a Fish.*

If animal companionship is your thing, at least have a pet that allows you to focus your efforts on the things that really matter: TV, sleep, and avoiding strenuous work. And what pet actually thrives on neglect? A fish.

Okay, they're not quite as lovable as a dog or a cat. But you can give them cool names like Mr. McGoldy, and watch them do tricks (mine can do *eat*, *crap*, and *swim*). And nothing seems to bother them – murky water, lack of friends, you being at work all day. So other than a cute, cuddly sloth, what's better than a murky-water, soulless, inert fish?

Step-by-step instructions:

1. Purchase your very own Mr. McGoldy from the local pet shop for a dollar.
2. Watch him eat, crap, and swim. And die.
3. Purchase Mr. McGoldy II.
4. Repeat.

* Assuming you've already adopted a sloth, which kicks ass!

*"**Collaboration**" comes from the Latin*
***Cola** – meaning 'thief,' and*
***Bora** – meaning 'good idea.'*

Way #42:
"Collaborate."

One of the best ways to get something accomplished at work with a minimum of effort is to have others come up with ideas you can claim as your own.

Step-by-step instructions:

1. Call a brainstorming session with your coworkers.

2. Have them generate lots of ideas, and assign someone to write them down on a white board (not you, that's way too much exertion).

3. Pick the best three and present them to your boss later (alone, of course).

4. Wait for your promotion.

The No-Guilt Twist™:

Remind yourself that it's better to give than to receive, so your coworkers are actually better off for helping you out.

The sloth at work.

Work from Your Home Office.

Ahh, working from home. It's sort of a holy grail for the sloth-minded – the prospect of having your entire life within a few feet of a couch, TV, and refrigerator.

Official Code Phrases When Working From Home (and What They Really Mean):

Official Code Phrase	*What you really mean*
"Sorry, I have an appointment."	...with the couch.
"Right now? I'm doing product research."	...on my Xbox 360.
"I'll be out-of-pocket until 6pm."	I'll be at the bar until I pass out.
"Tell the client we'll have to reschedule."	No way am I missing this episode of *Mad Men*.
"Of course, Dan. The report's nearly ready."	Hold on, I'm not done procrastinating.
"Sure, I can video conference in 10 minutes."	Crap. Now I have to wash my hair and put on a shirt.

"Mmm. Last Tuesday's meatloaf looks good."

Leave Leftovers in the Pot.

You're going to clean the pot anyway, right? So why sully a perfectly clean tupperware container for your leftovers, and then have to clean BOTH?

Step-by-step instructions:

1. Cook your entire meal in one pot. (Two or more pots? Does that even exist?)

2. Enjoy your meal. (Five extra points for eating right out of the pot.)

3. Put the leftover pot in the fridge. (Cover optional.)

4. Repeat step 2-4 every day until food is finished.

And Just For Good Measure™:

If you used your fingers to eat, you get an additional five points! (Wait – when did we start using points?)

Way #45:
Make a To-Do List.

Want to feel like you've accomplished something – without actually doing anything? Create a to-do list – the longer the better. You'll find that by simply writing down all the things you should be doing, you're sort of actually doing them (sort of).

Step-by-step instructions:

1. Make a really long to-do list.

2. Admire that you've gotten so organized.

3. Leave the list on the pile on your desk, and go out for a pulled pork sandwich.

The No-Guilt Twist™:

4. Make the first item on your to-do list "Create To-Do List" and check it off. See? *You're on fire, you go-getter!*

Stage 4:
Advanced Mastery.

(Okay, that sounds a little over-the-top. How about "Hey, you're getting pretty damn good at this.")

Sloths were considered teachers in ancient Rome.
(Okay, yes, I'm making most of these captions up.)

Way #46:
Become a Philosopher.

As you ~~walk~~ ~~crawl~~ sit on the journey to sloth, you'll meet people who don't share your view. That's when it's time to share this little fable:

> A jogger passes an old man walking slowly down a path. He slows down and says "Hey, you're not going to get anywhere going that slow." The old man says "We will both reach the same destination, will we not?" The first man says "Yeah, but I'll get there much quicker."
>
> Then the old man, a t'ai chi master, effortlessly snaps the other man's femur in three places. "We'll see about that."

Now, you may not change your friend's mind, but you definitely won't be getting any more crap about your life choices.

Way #47:
Sleep in Your Clothes.

Pajamas are for kids.

Okay, let's look at this Way logically: today you're wearing clothes. And tomorrow you'll be wearing clothes (I hope). So why do we put an extra change of clothes right in the middle of that, **just to go to bed tonight?** It's a waste of time, effort, laundry detergent, and water (assuming you eventually wash your sleepwear).

Step-by-step instructions:

1. Flop into bed with your clothes on. (Note: your bed shouldn't be made either, because that's also a waste of time.)

2. Get up at 3:00am to take your tie off. (This will stop that dream of a python strangling you.)

3. Wake up (checking for python under bed), and put your new clothes on for the day. *Look mom, no pajamas!*

For Advanced Learners Only:

4. Wake up and **don't** change your clothes. Are they really that dirty? (Note: signs of crotch rot will answer that question.)

Way #48:
Get an Apartment Above a Bar.

If you can stomach the noise late at night,
the smell of fried bar food, and occasionally
stepping in a puddle of vomit on your morning
walk to work, the benefits to this way are many:

- You'll save money, not needing to take cabs
  home stinking drunk

- You'll save time stumbling a shorter distance
  to bed

- It encourages Sleeping in Your Clothes
  (see previous Way)

- Fulfills your lifelong dream of living like
  Ernest Hemingway (just the drinking though,
  not the writing, marlin fishing, or bullfighting)

- BONUS: If you can work at the bar, you've
  eliminated a commute (and a career path)

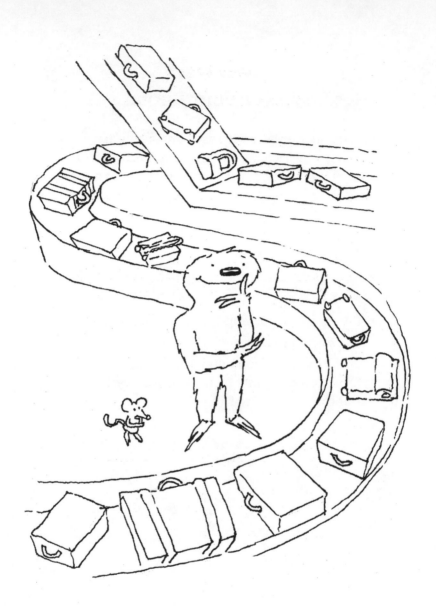

Way #49:

Check Your Bags.

Yes, it's nice to stop lugging your suitcases around an airport and let someone else worry about it. But that's not what makes this Way special – it's the endless waiting at the baggage carousel. Simply nirvana.

Step-by-step instructions:

1. Check your bags at the airport.

2. At your destination, go to the baggage pickup.

3. Slip into a standing coma watching the mesmerizing motion of the carousel, as it transports the same eighty-seven black bags (but not yours) in endless circles.

And Just For Good Measure™:

4. If you can muster the energy, count the number of times that bright pink duffle bag makes a full revolution before your bag finally comes around. (My record? A hundred and three.)

Way #50:

Hit The Snooze Button.

What feels better than cheating the productive world of another ten minutes and retreating into your own little mini-coma? *(Okay, maybe adopting a pet sloth. But other than that? Nothing.)*

Part of the perfection of this Way is the contradictory nature of the snooze button. Think about it: right on top of a machine that's supposed to wake you up is a big button that lets you sleep longer. And inexplicably, it's designed to be pressed as many times as you want. *Hooray for inventors!*

Step-by-step instructions:

1. Set your alarm clock for a full hour earlier than you need to get up.

2. When the alarm goes off, hit the snooze button and revel in the bliss of a perfect 10-minute hibernation.

3. Repeat for the full hour, then wake up in a panic and rush like hell to get to work on time.

Try This Experiment!™:

Set your alarm a few minutes earlier each night, allowing for even more smile-inducing dream sessions in the morning. Eventually, see if you can match my record: a full three hours of waking, tapping, and drifting back to oblivion.

Buy 20-Year Light Bulbs.

When they introduced these bad-boys this year, there was a big debate about the high cost, whether they're really good for the environment, whether the government should give tax credits for buying them, blah, blah, blah.

But here's the only fact that matters: after you expend all that energy getting out the step stool and screwing the new bulb in, IT WILL BE ANOTHER TWENTY YEARS UNTIL YOU HAVE TO DO IT AGAIN. *Now get back on that couch, hero!*

Step-by-step instructions:

1. Get out your step stool.

2. Replace your bulbs with 20-year bulbs.

3. Put your step stool away – **for two decades**.

Oh, And When You're Done™:

After you've switched, you've earned permission to use the following joke at will:
"Q: How many sloths does it take to screw in a light bulb?
A: I don't know – they still haven't finished."

Way #52:

Strive for an Ambiguous Job Title.

If no one really knows what you do at the office, you don't have to do anything! Here are some titles to keep in mind for your next position:

- Director of Internal Coordination
- Customer Sales Manager Resource Director
- Senior Assistant Project Facilitator
- Captain Whatsidoo
- Anything with the word "Liason"
- Vice President of the United States

Step-by-step instructions:

1. Obtain your Ambiguous Job Title
2. Wander in and out of offices and hallways all day, with a laptop in hand and a purposeful look on your face.
3. Delegate.
4. Go home.

Way #53:
Make Mac and Cheese.

If you asked a sloth what he makes for dinner, he'd say "reservations" *(insert rim shot sound effect here)*. But if you can't have someone else cook for you and clean up after you, what to make? Mac and Cheese – it's done in a couple of minutes, and it covers the four quadrants of the *Sloth Nutrition Food Cube™*: cheese, pasta, butter, and salt.

Of course, you should have a well-balanced diet (somebody told me that once), so here are more UtS-approved meals, recommended for their total lack of hassle, and minimal time investment:

- **Ham rolls:** put whatever you've got in the fridge (mustard, pickles, olives, old french fries) onto three open slices of ham cold cuts. Roll them up and enjoy! (Want to be extra fancy? Cut the rolls into slices like sushi and use chopsticks to eat them.)

- **Twinkies.** No preparation needed. Unwrap and gobble. Repeat until full. (Feel good about this one – the white filling looks creamy, and cream contains calcium, which is good for you.)

- **Dominos.** Pick up phone. Answer front door. Mounch.

Way #54:

Develop an Intense
Fear of Driving.

My dad actually inspired this Way. After his
heart surgery, he basically refused to drive
for the rest of his life on the fear he might die
behind the wheel – and has been chauffeured
around like Miss Daisy by my mom ever since.
Thanks for the idea, Pop!

Way #55:

Daydream.

Wikipedia: "Daydreaming is a short-term detachment from one's immediate surroundings, during which a person's contact with reality is blurred and partially substituted by a visionary fantasy, especially one of happy, pleasant thoughts, hopes or ambitions, imagined as coming to pass, and experienced while awake."

Me: "...Wha? Huh? Oh, yeah, I was totally just paying attention... What was the question?"

Way #56:

Stare Off Into Space.

Yes, it's as valuable as daydreaming, but requiring even LESS effort – no hassle of actually having to come up with some hope or ambition to think about. Just revel in the utter blankness of your mind.

Sponging off your parents can foster
extremely high levels of enlightenment.

Way #57:
Live With Your Parents.

Though I no longer live with my parents, I often ask myself "Why the hell not? Am I an idiot?"

A Pro/Con Analysis of Living With Your Parents:

PROS:

- Free rent
- Free food
- Free TV and Internet
- Free use of laundry (or better yet, see if you can swing Mom doing your laundry)
- No curfew
- "Loans" (quotes mean repayment is optional)
- You'll always be their baby (Maybe not your Dad - he might want you to get the hell out)

CONS:

- Parents can be annoying ("Dinner NOW, Mom? I'm right in the middle of *Cake Boss!*")
- Can't bring random friends home without interrogation the following morning
- Mom can keep your room TOO clean

I hope it's obvious: the cons are a small price to pay for the level of sloth-like enlightenment you'll achieve mooching off your folks.

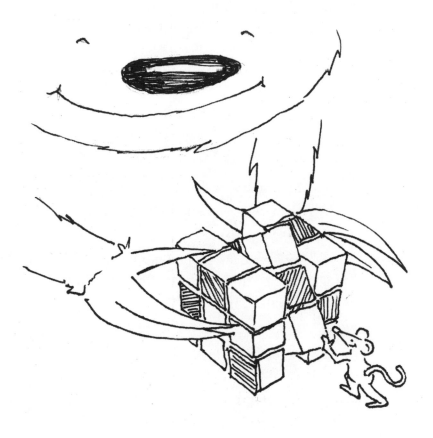

Solving the world's most popular braniac puzzle?
Or just randomly flipping little colored cubes to
impress someone? Either way, you win.

Way #58:

Get Really Interested in Rubik's Cube.

This game is awesome – it SEEMS like an academic pursuit, like mathematics. And it can be. But it's also an excellent way to look like you're doing something smart.

Step-by-step instructions:

1. Pick up the cube while you're watching TV.

2. Idly turn the sides and look at it occasionally. (Be careful not to interrupt your focus on *Goodfellas* – there are too many good parts)

3. Smile knowingly as you astonish your friends and family with your focus, analytical skills, and determination.

The No-Guilt Twist™:

Okay, you may not really be exercising your mind, but you're definitely working out your finger muscles. (*Those TV remote buttons aren't going to press themselves, people!*)

Way #59:

Move to a Place
Where it Snows a Lot.

It's a fact: snow gives you permission to hibernate. So the logic follows – why not move to Alaska? Or better yet, Siberia?

Official List of Things You <u>Don't</u> Have to Do When It Snows:

- Go to school
- Go to work
- Mow the lawn
- Go outside
- Call your parents *(the telephone lines are probably down, I won't even bother checking)*
- Clean your home *(who's going to schlep over here in this weather?)*
- Go food shopping *(it's treacherous out there!)*
- Cook *(Snow means entering survival mode, which means eating junk food from the pantry)*
- Move from the couch

Way #60:

Facebook.

Get ready to update your status to "enlightened," folks – because Facebook is quite possibly the ultimate tool to find yourself. (And by *"find yourself"* I mean *"find yourself wasting hours at a time without realizing it."*)

Step-by-step instructions:

1. Go online to your Facebook page.

2. Enjoy news from your friends, like:

   • Why they hate Mondays – again.

   • How their cup of coffee was this morning.

   • How their child can do this amazing thing, proving (again) that they're an amazing parent.

   • How they're helping a cause by reposting other people's repostings.

   • Inspirational quotes. *(Most of which remind you to get out there and enjoy life – while you're sitting there hunched over your laptop.)*

3. Three hours later, return to the real world, swearing Facebook is a complete waste of your precious time, and you're not going back.

4. Ten minutes later, check for updates.

Stage 5:
Unleash the Sloth!

Sloths move extremely slowly on land – except when they're tooling around on kick-ass scooters like this one.

Way #61:

Get Old.

Yes, it'll take years to complete this Way, but BOY will it be worth it. Here's a list of things you'll be able to get away with when you're a crotchety old coot:

- Napping 18 hours a day *(just like an actual sloth)*

- Making no effort to filter what you think before you say it. *("Thank goodness you don't look anything like his last girlfriend. She was a trollop. Well, I hope you're not a trollop anyway.")*

- Walking? Not when you've got a bitchin' Rascal scooter to do the walking for you!

- Watching record amounts of TV *(My dad can go for nine hours before he realizes my mom is locked out of the house and lets her in.)*

- Work? A distant, fading memory.

- Having other people hold doors open for you. Booyah! *(Wait, do old people say Booyah?)*

Way #62:
Develop Writer's Block.

"Attention passengers for flight 402 to Boston: please
wait for another hour in the gate area, until we cancel
the flight at the last moment. Thank you."

Way #63:

Take Lots of Business Trips.

This one sounds wrong, but between the moments of actual productivity on business trips are the **endless hours** of non-productive time, welcoming you like a eucalyptus tree welcomes the great sloth.

Sample Business Trip Timeline:

4:00am	Wake up. *(After hitting snooze button for an hour – see Way #50)*
4:30am	Wait for taxi to airport.
5:30am	Wait in security line *(see Way #6)*.
6:00am	Wait at gate.
8:00am	Sit on airplane for three hours.
11:00am	Wait for luggage. *(Enjoy memsmerizing baggage carousel – See Way #49)*
11:00am	Wait for taxi to hotel.
11:30am	Wait for guy at hotel front desk to finish giving elderly couple directions to Denny's.
12:00pm	Wait for taxi to meeting.
12:30pm	Wait for meeting to start.
1:00pm	**ACTUAL PRODUCTIVE MEETING.**
3:00pm	Wait for taxi back to hotel.
4:00pm	Wait for client to show up for dinner...

...And on, and on, and on, for a couple of days. *Let the waiting begin!*

Way #64:

Be Forgetful.

As you follow the Ways of the Sloth, it can be very helpful to have a poor memory. The effort it can save you is **tremendous**:

- "Honey, I'm sorry, I forgot to mow the lawn. And now it's raining. Darn."

- "Oops. I forgot to do my homework. For the whole semester."

- "On your way home can you pick up the dry cleaning? I totally forgot. Oh, and pick me up a nice throw while you're out."

- "Now how did I forget to go to work today?"

- "Wait, I forget – am I supposed to be writing this book, or napping? Oh yeah – napping."

Way #64:
Be Forgetful.

As you follow the Ways of the Sloth, it can be very helpful to have a poor memory. Wait - did I write this one already?

Way #64:
Be Forgetful.

Sorry, I had to do it one more time.
I swear I won't do it again.

Way #65:
Don't Repeat Yourself Too Often.

A-Ha! You thought I was going to say "Be Forgetful" again, right?

A true sloth master, like a black belt in karate, must not make his methods obvious, lest his weaknesses be revealed. **No, grasshopper, you must be forever diligent!** (Wait, that sounds like a lot of work. Just be sort of diligent.) Like this:

- Just when a co-worker is about to say "Hey, wasn't it your birthday last month?" keel over, grab your chest, and scream "My heart!" They'll forget instantly. (And you'll get at least a week off from work.)

- After selling your third completely blank canvas as an art masterpiece (see Way #38), spill a little red paint on the fourth. Rather than dismiss you as a repetitive hack, critics will pronounce you've entered your "Color Period."

- After you've "forgotten" to mow the lawn four weeks in a row, don't attempt a fifth. Instead, tell your significant other that you've had a brainstorm – growing grass as an edible crop! (Obviously it needs to grow a few feet tall before you can harvest it, right?)

Way #66:
Listen to One Radio Station.

Have you ever spent an **entire** car ride shuffling through your presets or trying to find something good on the radio? Such wasted effort, young apprentice!

The solution is simple: find one station and **lock it in**. Period. Forever. (This means, of course, that you'll still be listening to it when they change the format from classic rock to celtic bagpipes. Sorry.)

If You Must Have a Hobby Other Than Watching TV...

- **Orchids.**
  This may be the ultimate sloth hobby, because you don't actually do anything except water them once every six weeks. And they sort of look okay even when they die.

- **Zen Rock Gardening.**
  This hobby is all about minimalism. Pour some sand into your garden, throw a few rocks in, strategically place your rake, then sit back with a burrito and soak it all in. *Ommm.*

- **Bird Watching.**
  Wait. *Hey, I see one!* Wait. *Hey, I see one!* Wait.

- **Collecting Precious Moments Figurines.**
  You collect them. They collect dust.

Way #68:
Use Only Consonants.

Imgn hw mch nrgy y cn cnsrv by wrtng wth n vwls!

Way #69:

Take a Thirty-Minute Shower.

It's worth repeating: *Unleash the Sloth* isn't about becoming lazy – it's about doing more of what you want, and less of what you don't.

Take the act of showering. Why get out when you're clean? Instead, reward the fine five-minute work you've done ridding yourself of B.O. with another twenty-five minutes of warm, wet bliss.

"Wait – you missed a spot."

Way #70:
Fill Your Work Area With Framed Fake Certificates.

Nothing says "I'm legitimate" like a wall full of diplomas. Trot out this look, and workmates will assume you're a real go-getter (even though the only thing you're trying to "go-get" is leaving work early.)

"But where can I find a variety of real-looking B.S. certificates?" you ask. As usual, *Unleash The Sloth* brings it to you effortlessly:

1. Go online and close your Facebook page.

2. Visit **www.unleashthesloth.com** and click on the **UtS *Fake Certificates*™** link.

3. Print out as many as will fit –the more crammed your wall the better. And they're FREE!

4. PLEASE don't forget to put them in frames. Nothing says "I'm faking it" like a bunch of photocopies scotch-taped to your wall.

Way #71:

Eat With Your Fingers.

You don't see a sloth using a fork and knife, do you? They understand that utensils are just an obstacle between food and your mouth. (Also, have you seen their claws? Good luck.)

Benefits of eating with your fingers:

- Save effort not lifting heavy utensils
- Save money not buying utensils
- Save time not cleaning utensils
- Save food for later under your fingernails

Oh, And Just In Case™:

Having soup? The bowl **IS** the utensil!

Way #72:

Think Disposable.

If you find yourself still using utensils for some strange reason *(to avoid being shunned by your own family, for example)*, start thinking disposable. Because anything you have to actually clean is a royal pain in the ass.

Some idea starters:

- Disposable utensils

- Disposable clothing *(as long as you don't mind wearing hospital gowns all the time)*

- Disposable appliances *(done with that pot of coffee? Smash it in the fireplace – don't worry, it's a Greek tradition!)*

- Disposable linens *(use paper towels – yes, even for your bedsheets)*

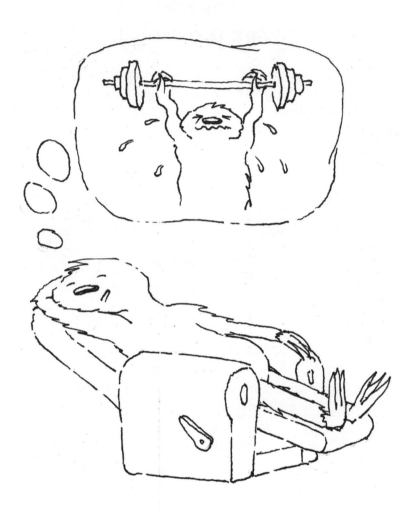

Way #73:
Join the Gym.

Yes, it's another Way that sounds paradoxical. But the trick here is to keep workouts as a **potential**, not as a **reality**.

Step-by-step instructions:

1. Join the gym.

2. Smile, knowing that *tomorrow* is the day you'll start on the road to an active lifestyle. Definitely. No prisoners. *I will do it!*

3. Repeat step 2 every day for the rest of your life.

The No-Guilt Twist™:

Hey, at least you didn't buy a treadmill, too. (Wait, you didn't buy a treadmill, too, did you?)

Way #74:
Move Stuff Around.

Like an expert magician, a true disciple of sloth makes use of the art of misdirection to create his illusion (in this case the illusion that you're actually doing something). Some examples:

At work:

Anywhere you go at the office, bring your laptop and a bunch of important-looking papers. In fact, as the day progresses, keep adding stuff to the load. By the end of the day, coworkers should barely be able to see the top of your face when you walk by. Then bring it all back to your office, plop it down, and go home.

At dinner *(I swear we actually did this one when we were kids - sorry, Mom)***:**

Move your finished plate to the sink area. Then into the sink. Then back to the table like you forgot something. Repeat until you get caught.

In the yard:

Buy a bush for your garden. Put it in a wheelbarrow and bring it to the perfect spot. Then decide it should go next to the shed. Then bring it out to the front yard. Then back to the garden. Repeat. By the time you're done, it'll be raining, and you can go inside and watch the football game without having lifted a single shovelful of dirt.

Like Yourself.

Yes, I've included a completely serious Way in this book – in fact, the only one you really need:

It's okay to be you.

Now, it's also good to try to improve yourself, take charge of your life, make a good living, and all that. But don't beat yourself up for watching a little too much TV, or slacking a bit at work, or napping while your kids are outside playing. Just remember the smiling face of the sloth, hanging in the trees, being himself, and knowing that all is well.

Unleash the Sloth!
Quick-Reference Cheat Sheet

You think I want you to REMEMBER all this stuff?
Or worse yet, have to read it all over again?

Not on my watch.

That's what a cheat sheet is for. Now any time
you're feeling burdened, stressed, or just don't
feel like doing something your boss/wife/
husband/mom/dad/coworker is asking you to
do, whip this out and ask yourself "Which of
these Ways is the easiest to do, yet will be most
effective? What would a sloth do?"

Stage 1: Learning to Hang.

Way #1: Procrastinate.
Way #2: Have At Least Forty Hobbies.
Way #3: Nap. (a.k.a. "meditation")
Way #4: Don't Sort Your Laundry.
Way #5: Put Clothes Directly from Dryer to Drawer.
Way #6: Wait in Line.
Way #7: Double-space your work.
Way #8: Take Short Cuts.
Way #9: Get Sick.
Way #10: Do All Your Research on Wikipedia.
Way #11: Sleep In.
Way #12: Duck Responsibility.
Way #13: Replace Your Signature with an "X."
Way #14: Do You REALLY Want Kids?
Way #15: Teach Your Kids the Ways.
Way #16: Give All Your Kids The Same Name.

Stage 2: Drifting Off.

Way #17: Watch TV.
Way #18: Be Apathetic.
Way #19: Use Cruise Control Only.
Way #20 Play Video Games.
Way #21: Jaywalk.
Way #22: Adopt a Sloth.
Way #23: Shower Once a Week.
Way #24: Eliminate All Exercise.
Way #25: Attend an Unleash The Sloth Workshop.
Way #26: Text Message.
Way #27: Go to the Movies.
Way #28: Get a Refrigerator For Your Cubicle.
Way #29: Make Believe It's Your Birthday.
Way #30: Don't Go To Work Today.
Way #31: Don't Go To Work Ever Again.

Stage 3: The Sloth Mind.

Way #32: Google.
Way #33: Remove All the Doorknobs in Your House.
Way #34: Remove All the DOORS in Your House.
Way #35: Go to Church.
Way #36: Enjoy a Sunset.
Way #37: Go fishing.
Way #38: Become a Minimalist Painter.
Way #39: Buy Yourself a Nice Throw.
Way #40: Set Your Pet Free.
Way #41: If You Must Have a Pet, Get a Fish.
Way #42 "Collaborate."
Way #43: Work from Your Home Office.
Way #44: Leave Leftovers in the Pot.
Way #45: Make a To-Do List.

Stage 4: Advanced Mastery.

Way #46: Become a Philosopher.
Way #47: Sleep in Your Clothes.
Way #48: Get an Apartment Above a Bar.
Way #49: Check Your Bags.
Way #50: Hit The Snooze Button.
Way #51: Buy 20-Year Light Bulbs.
Way #52: Strive for an Ambiguous Job Title.
Way #53: Make Mac and Cheese.
Way #54: Develop an Intense Fear of Driving.
Way #55: Daydream.
Way #56: Stare Off Into Space.
Way #57: Live With Your Parents.
Way #58: Get Really Interested in Rubik's Cube.
Way #59: Move to a Place Where it Snows a Lot.
Way #60: Facebook.

Stage 5: Unleash the Sloth!

Way #61: Get Old.
Way #62: Develop Writer's Block.
Way #63: Take Lots of Business Trips.
Way #64: Be Forgetful.
Way #65: Don't Repeat Yourself Too Often.
Way #66: Listen to One Radio Station.
Way #67: If You Must Have a Hobby Other Than TV...
Way #68: Use Only Consonants.
Way #69: Take a Thirty-Minute Shower.
Way #70: Fill Your Work Area With Fake Certificates.
Way #71: Eat With Your Fingers.
Way #72: Think Disposable.
Way #73: Join the Gym.
Way #74: Move Stuff Around.
Way #75: Like Yourself.

WAIT! BONUS!
Way #76:
Don't Finish What You Start.

You've completed your coursework, and mastered the Ways of the enigmatic sloth. So you've earned a peek at the ultimate, hidden secret to nirvana, the full mystery revealed...

Its...

Why stop now? There's more online.

www.unleashthesloth.com

- **Adopt a Sloth.** Okay, it's not a real one, but honestly you won't be able to tell the difference. Adopt (and by adopt I mean purchase) your very own super-high quality plush sloth doll, custom *Unleash the Sloth!* t-shirt, and certificate of adoption (complete with unique name). He also comes with a complimentary copy of the book – making him the perfect gift for the sloth in your life.

- **Get Gear.** Wear your accomplishments in the Ways with pride. I've plastered inspiring sloth-related phrases on everything: T-shirts, hats, buttons, coffee mugs – you name it.

- **Add Your OWN Way.** Now I KNOW that while you were reading this book, you thought of something I missed – and you're right. There are tons more Ways waiting to be revealed, by YOU. Go to the site and add your own, and rate the Ways submitted by other readers.

- **Get FREE Stuff.** Throughout the book, I've mentioned things you can get online (frameable fake certificates, for example). Well, it wasn't a joke – you can actually go online and download it all FREE.

Also from Rob Dircks...

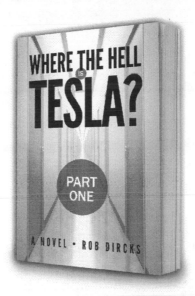

SCI-FI ODDYSEY.
COMEDY. LOVE STORY.
AND THAT'S JUST PART ONE.

I found the journal at work. Well, I don't know if you'd call it work, but that's where I found it. It's the lost journal of Nikola Tesla, one of the greatest inventors and visionaries ever. Before he died in 1943, he kept a notebook filled with spectacular claims and outrageous plans. One of these plans was for an "Interdimensional Transfer Apparatus" – that allowed someone (in this case me and my friend Pete) to travel to other versions of the infinite dimensions that make up the multiverse. Crazy, right? But that's just where the crazy starts.

// Will appeal to fans of Pratchett and Adams. //

★★★★ Amazon Review

Available at www.robdircks.com

Acknowledgements

Thanks to Kellie Dircks for living through my "research."

Thanks to Dave Dircks for the awesome illustrations.

Thanks to Ken Dircks and Chris Dircks for contributing.

Made in the USA
Lexington, KY
17 April 2015